TEACH YOURSELF OR YOUR CHIL
AT HOME WITHOUT A PO(

TEACH YOURSELF TO SW
e-Book Series
IN ONE MINUTE STEPS

"You can easily transfer these familiar motor skills to the shallow end of a pool or lake on a weekend or summer trip"

By

DR. PETE ANDERSEN

http://www.LearnToSwimProgram.com

http://bit.ly/FaceBook-LearnToSwimProgram

http://bit.ly/YouTube-LearnToSwimProgram

https://www.Pinterest.com/LearnToSwimProg

www.SwimVideoCoach.com

www.YouTube.com/SwimVideoCoach

www.TeachYourselfToSwim.com

Your comments and www.Amazon.com reviews are welcome.

JOIN OUR MISSION TO HELP SAVE MORE LIVES!!!

Enjoy and pass along what you learn to others

Trius Publishing, P.O. Box 600801, San Diego, CA 92160

TEACH YOURSELF OR YOUR CHILD TO SWIM AT HOME WITHOUT A POOL

List of paperback / Kindle books and DVD sets in the

TEACH YOURSELF TO SWIM series -
IN ONE MINUTE STEPS [or Your Child] TO SWIM

ISBN # / ASIN #   Title

ISBN # / ASIN #	Title
978-0-9820248-7-4 B00TSV32EC	TEACH YOURSELF OR YOUR CHILD TO SWIM AT HOME WITHOUT A POOL
978-0-9820248-2-9 B00TXWW284	TEN BEST STEPS TEACHING YOURSELF TO SWIM SAFELY AND EFFICIENTLY
978-0-9820248-8-1 B01CYYTQPO	FLOATING RELAXED
978-0-9820248-9-8 B01CZK84FK	FREESTYLE WITH BREATHING
978-0-9899468-0-3 B01CZK8971	USING YOUR OWN FEEDBACK
978-0-9899468-1-0 B01CZLEH2S	USING SIX NEW TEACHING METHODS
978-0-9899468-2-7 B01CZLERQY	BACKSTROKE THE EASY WAY
978-0-9899468-3-4 B01CZM0KU0	WATER SAFETY CONCERNS IN OTHER ENVIRONMENTS
978-0-9899468-4-1 B01CZMM846	WATER SAFETY RESTING SKILLS
978-0-9899468-5-8 B01D0EO3VO	IN DEEP WATER WITHOUT FEAR
978-0-9899468-6-5 B01D0FA7S6	SHALLOW TO DEEP WATER PROGRESSION
978-0-9899468-7-2 B01D0FABI2	ELEMENTARY BACKSTROKE FOR SAFETY
978-0-9899468-8-9 B01D0FP9HU	BREASTSTROKE THE EASY WAY
978-0-9899468-9-6 B01D0G7VDY	ADVANCED WORKOUT SKILLS
978-0-9820248-3-6	Active Lifestyle (3 DVD set 5 hours 37 minutes)
978-0-9820248-4-3	Parents, Grandparents, Beginners, Non-Swimmers, Instructors (4 DVD set 7 hours 24 minutes)
978-0-9820248-5-0	Competitor Masters, Senior Olympians, Triathletes, Age-Group Swimmers (2 DVD set 3 hours 21 minutes)

TBD/ASIN	Ten Best Steps Teaching Yourself to Swim Safely and Efficiently
	(1 DVD 1 hour 15 minutes)

Series of single DVD disks of the same content as the e-books is being completed as of this printing. They will be available on Amazon and my shopping cart for under $10.

 See fast link below.

You can order from

www.Amazon.com/Books

www.Amazon.com/Videos

OR   order directly from the website

www.LearnToSwimProgram.com

shopping cart using the fast link:

 http://bit.ly/1NdevtV

Most of these are under $10 to get you started.

Author's Personal Message of Introduction

In August of 2010 I heard a news report of nine related African-American teens that drowned in the Arkansas River trying to rescue each other. My emotion immediately shifted to thinking how I would feel losing one of my six kids or now thirteen grandchildren.

I sat down in a chair and cried for about twenty minutes. And then I got mad thinking how could teenagers not even know how to make a human chain to interlock wrists to wade in and rescue someone in a current?

That thought prompted another, "How can we teach people to swim in rural and low income areas where there is no pool or an experienced instructor like to me to show them how they can teach themselves to swim?" For the past 50 plus years since I learned to teach swimming as a high school freshman and went on to earn my B.S. and M.S. teaching degrees in health and physical education at Indiana University I have monitored the evolution of swimming instruction.

At Indiana I was also a 5-time NCAA Division I All-American coached by the legend Doc Counsilman who later coached Mark Spitz and our winningest 1964 and 1976 U.S. Men's Olympic Swimming Teams and a string of six NCAA Championships.

From Doc and my teaching degrees I learned how to apply all the physics principles to learn to swim instruction. At the same time to finance my graduate degrees I was a Director of Aquatics for Country Clubs and a large Chicago suburban high school and park district of 80,000 people. I directed and trained all our high school student instructors to teach swimming to our community grade school children in our Saturday morning and summer swim school programs.

Before I started in my first teaching and head coaching position I had already been teaching swimming for ten years. But after four more years gaining valuable director experience running large programs I felt I needed more knowledge.

I went back to graduate school to earn my Ph.D. in psychology of learning principles with emphasis in behavioral and educational psychology and statistical analysis. I completed a three year program in two years because I was allowed to collect dissertation data while I was attending classes.

Another reason was because my wife at the time and I had triplet boys born three months into my program to add to my three-year-old son. Between helping at home bathe, feed, and change diapers, and going to

5

classes and teaching classes as a grad assistant I only got an average of four hours sleep.

With my swimming pedigree the University put me in charge of teaching most of the college swimming courses. And for my dissertation I tested our 1972 U.S. Men's Olympic Swim Team and six of the top ten NCAA Division I teams.

All throughout my degreed programs it was impressed on all students to embrace professional growth - to keep learning. Over the years teaching thousands to swim and hundreds to be quality instructors I found that my students taught me!

I would change my method or cue and see how they would respond to learn that skill faster. Later now in my book and videos I have introduced six new teaching methods no other instructor or program is using.

I had already added physics principles and now added psychology of learning principles from my Ph.D. I've learned that no other instructor in the world has achieved. Coupled with having swum and been a 5-time All-American mentored by the greatest swim coach of all time I am blessed with very good skills.

Using these skills and my desire to prove my system of easy-to-master one minute steps gets faster longer-lasting results, I got back into competitive swimming with the U.S. Masters Swimming. It took six years of training to set my first World Record, and since I've always been in the top 10 in the U.S. and FINA World Rankings for my age group. I have also achieved 21 Senior Olympic Summer Games Championships Gold Medals with records to match.

I like to tell people it's not like I'm a man telling a woman how to have a baby. I practice and prove what I teach every day. My proven results and ability means I know how to correctly demonstrate and teach the correct visual, verbal, and most important kinesthetic or feeling cues with imagery techniques to speed up the learning process.

My system is now proven to get faster longer-lasting results because it follows a system of sequential steps to make it easier for the brain to learn. The imagery cues I use are universal to children and adults like floating level as an air mattress, or reaching over a barrel or a ball to get your hand catch and arm rotation correct for example.

In the summer of 2010 when those nine teens drowned I took action and sat down to write up a sequential curriculum for all the strokes. I also wanted to write in simple terms to explain how never out-of-date physics and psychology of learning principles would be applied so people could learn to teach themselves to swim with my correct pictures demonstrating the skills.

This would really help save more lives especially in rural and low income areas or when people had large families. I reasoned that 1) learning to swim is a necessity and the only sport that has the potential to save your life, and 2) water has a way of finding you when you are least prepared that can lead to panic and a tragic result.

Eventually I became an expert in drowning prevention and swimming instruction to do radio interviews all over the U.S. My book and the only complete video curriculum instructional series in the world to include all the strokes plus water safety concerns in unfamiliar places were published.

I believed all major swim programs would embrace my work as "the new science of swimming instruction" for professional growth to upgrade their swimming instruction. All my content is based on irrefutable physics and psychology of learning principles. We all support the universal mission to save more lives.

But that has not happened. Instead they have rebuked my efforts to protect "their brand" as a sort of sacred cow. And perhaps for this reason alone the unintentional drowning death rate has not come down.

All the major organizations have proved very protective and unwilling to change. Therein lays the most significant problem why unintentional drowning deaths have not declined in the last few decades.

In my analysis getting all my fairly reliable statistics from the Atlanta based Centers for Disease Control and Prevention or CDC there are still on average ten unintentional drowning deaths each day in the U.S. and many more in other countries. The most likely reason is there are no pools or experienced instructors.

There are cultural issues and myths to overcome. As reported by the CDC 70% of blacks and 60% of Hispanics do not know how to swim. The worst myth is that blacks have heavier bones and smaller lungs and cannot float. What a lie that is!

In the 1000's I've taught to swim I've only had two black males who were body builders with only 6% body fat that were negatively buoyant. But I still taught them how to swim.

If the mother does not know how to swim their child has only a 13% chance of learning how to swim. But if a child learns to swim before the age of four they have an 88% chance of surviving a water accident.

Now you can see the importance I place on teaching parents how to start teaching their babies to swim at home without a pool at 2-18 months when they bathe them. Is this process any harder than teaching their kids to learn and improve a backyard sports skill to transfer to the playing field or court?

I try to change all that at home without a pool using their kitchen sink, dressing mirror, mattress, and a bathtub. Now they can get familiar with all the basic physical motor patterns at home without fear of drowning.

Then when they learn at their own pace and feel confident they can transfer those same familiar skills to the shallow end of a pool or lake where they can stand up. I even teach people how to float with their mouth open to make a better air lock with their nose and how to use goggles to see the pool bottom to place their feet and stand up!

When a lot of people live in rural areas or have large families and cannot afford pool admission or lessons my "TEACH YOURSELF TO SWIM" system helps solve this growing problem to help save more lives.

Rather than waste any more time with other swimming instructional organizations and programs I have elected to use technology and social media to reach out to people in need to save them time and money and frustration.   All my content is available on Amazon, select bookstores and swim outlet stores, and my website www.LearnToSwimProgram.com or shop directly using this link http://bit.ly/1NdevtV

I've learned that kids like adults don't like to waste their time when they are not learning from young inexperienced instructors who cannot demonstrate or teach with correct methods and cues because they are not being taught how to teach by the organizations. They make certification a joke in the U.S., but not in Australia or New Zealand where I have visited and had meetings with their organization directors. You have to prove your ability to teach before they will certify you.

The result is that most of the kids taking lessons today never master their rhythmical breathing to swim continuously any distance to save their life. Even their floating skills are poor. And worse, they never learn about wave actions, currents, marine life, and hypothermia to avoid risks.

The #1 reason why people unintentionally drown is because they overestimate their swimming ability. Most learn in a clear heated pool with goggles. And once they pass a minimal test they are cleared to have fun and go off the diving boards in the deep well. So they think they are good enough swimmers because they can make it from the diving board to the ladder.

But that won't help them in an ocean rip or river current or fast moving stream in a flood. Boys and young men are the worst at getting their macho ego involved to overestimate their ability. So I created the mental skills swim test.

Sit down in a chair and close your eyes. Now imagine swimming out into a lake 100 yards where you cannot see the bottom and the water is only 70 degrees. That's only the length of a football field. Okay now rest a bit and swim back.

If you took a gasp or deeper than normal breathing cycle, or your heart rate started to increase slightly, then you are not as good a swimmer as you think you are. Kids on swim teams would have no problem doing that.

Of the ten people who unintentionally drown each day two are children generally under the age of four. But the other eight are adults! What percentage of those eight adults probably took lessons as kids? So why has the number not been declining.

Could it be that large organizations are not willing to upgrade their swimming teaching methods and cues to reflect the new science applying physics and psychology of learning principles?

That is what I am all about and have proven results so you can benefit from in the contents of my work producing a book and video curriculum series. I believe I can teach you better on your own TV or downloading my chapters to your tablet to take to the pool or lake than any young inexperienced teacher.

And now for the first time I have created a series of e-books, paperbacks, and video disks devoted to only one smaller part of the curriculum at a time to make it even more affordable for everyone to teach themselves.

My system of easy-to-master one minute steps is embedded in each product's content so you can get faster longer-lasting results, save money, time, and most important improve the overall safety of your family.

After you invest and use any of my products I'd like to learn your comments. You are also going to get a series of three "fast-start" tutorials for free you can forward to all your friends and family on emails and links to the tutorials on your social media. Together we can help save more lives.

Sincerely,

Pete Andersen, Ph.D.

For free swim tips www.LearnToSwimProgram.com/Swim-Tips

or use this link http://bit.ly/1NdevtV to shop

*** FREE BONUS OFFER ***

Get valuable FREE content. Forward a copy of your Amazon Kindle book receipt to: drpete@LearnToSwimProgram.com OR ... complete the easy form on my website www.LearnToSwimProgram.com/Subscribe OR ...

 Scan the code or text or voice mail your name and email to 1-858-886-9820
               and
I will give you my download to my

Best Selling e-book valued at $9.97
"Teach Yourself or Your Kids to Swim
at Home Without a Pool"

AND

My popular nine page article
"Tips to Prevent Drowning"

AND

Get three valuable "Fast-Start" tutorials & podcasts

AND

Please provide your book review. Get the fast link from

http://www.LearnToSwimProgram.com/Amazon-Reviews

Find us on

http://bit.ly/FaceBook-LearnToSwimProgram

http://bit.ly/YouTube-LearnToSwimProgram

https://www.Pinterest.com/LearnToSwimProg

www.LinkedIn.com/In/DrPeteAndersen

www.Twitter.com/DrPeteAndersen

To give me permission to send you
VALUABLE FREE content, or
go to leave a comment or ask your question:

http://www.LearnToSwimProgram.com/Contact-Form

and submit the easy form

****

To find out how to achieve all your
swimming strokes, water safety
and more, go to:

http://www.LearnToSwimProgram.com/Resources

The following contents are listed for you to choose
your level of interest.

Would you benefit from more quality **FREE CONTENT** tips, webinars, and videos to get faster longer lasting results?

Could your Age-Group or Masters Swimming Teams benefit from a $3,000 - $7,500 easy "turn-key" program **FUNDRAISER**?

Would you like to be rewarded for recommending our quality books/DVDs to your family, relatives, friends, neighbors, co-workers, teammates, using your e-mail and social media? Then be sure to sign up for our **AFFILIATES** program? It's easy.

Would you like to continue improving your water safety knowledge and swimming skills in a monthly **GROUP MEMBERSHIP** that meets every other week, gives you more resources, and can get all your questions answered?

Do you desire All-American level **PERSONAL COACHING** to take your skills and fitness to the next level with Skype?

Would your organization, association, corporation, or team benefit from one of my professional instructional **CLINICS**?

Would you like to join our mission to save more lives by qualifying to become an **AMBASSADOR** and enjoy getting valuable discounts on books, DVDs, clinics, group membership, and personal coaching?

Imagine enjoying swimming better with family and friends. It's easy with my easy-to-master one minute steps system.

Imagine saving your money and time and getting faster longer lasting results from a pro instructor! Then if you take local lessons you'll get more out of them.

To find out how to achieve all these things and more, go to:

http://www.LearnToSwimProgram.com/Resources

TABLE OF CONTENTS

Ch. 1   Change your mindset to think positive

There are short chapters in this e-book. There are easy-to-master steps as you progress in a number sequence that is capitalized sub titles. You now have the opportunity to learn a variety of swimming skills, and not just freestyle. Floating is an essential skill few beginners or even advanced competitive swimmers take time to master. But you should. If you think you know how to perform all these skills, guess again. Just do them in sequence to know for sure and build your confidence. Mastery is a challenge to keep learning and perfecting all your swimming skills. Take this e-book with you to the pool and learn all the steps in stages, a few or many at a time depending on your current skill level.

This illustrated book with sequence pictures is changing the marketing strategy for teaching swimming worldwide. People have been conditioned to believe they cannot teach themselves or others how to swim because they think they need a pool or body of water to learn the basic skills. My aim is to bring swimming instruction into the home or public arena where there is no pool or body of water nearby, then show you how you can easily transfer the same identical elements of the basic motor patterns learned at home to shallow water in a safer environment.

You can build basic swimming skills as motor patterns in the brain in your own home using a kitchen sink, dressing mirror, bed, and bathtub as easily as learning to play and catch balls in your back yard. With your help my social media marketing approach will reach more people and save more lives.

There are several reasons why ten people drown each day in the United States. The biggest reason is that under the current marketing system, you have to live in metropolitan areas with pools to find instructional programs. And then you are not assured of an excellent curriculum, experienced instructors, and teaching methods and cues that get faster results. People living in rural areas or low socio economic status suffer graver consequences.

If you were not provided with instruction when you were a child, it's hard to find an adult class. Young and inexperienced instructors do not feel comfortable teaching adults because they can't think like an adult. They worry about having to make a save or performing mouth-to-mouth if an adult should happen to suffer a heart attack from over exertion caused by swimming inefficiently, and not floating very well.

You know your children should learn how to be safe around water when you go on vacations, but realize an average private swim lesson will cost you $20 per half hour or is marketed as a book of five lessons for $100. Instead of taking the time to master the basics at home to get more out of those lessons, you watch a young instructor beg your four-year-old to put his face in the water for the first 15 minutes. Cha-ching ten bucks! Forget that you have 2, 3, or 4 other children who also need lessons.

Maybe $100 is not a problem for you, but this amount poses a serious problem worldwide for low income families who can't afford even the pool admission. But those parents want to protect their children, too. I want to help more people easily learn how with better skills for as little cost as possible.

This book introduces new methods of swimming instruction based on the science of physics and psychology of learning principles. My marketing plan is to get this book and video series interpreted into as many foreign languages as possible. I will make the program available through foreign government distribution to their masses to save more lives. Social media, affiliates, and joint venture partners will also play a critical role to reach more people worldwide.

This is not a franchise that has a limited market based on profit with little quality control. There is no costly recurring franchise, pool membership, or lesson fees that can be as high as $1,000's of dollars. Everyone who invests in this book for under $20 and/or adds the videos for a package of $97 can continue to review and share in this resource with your family and friends. Perhaps you could encourage your local library to make this investment, and your whole community or school system can check it out and reach more people.

Water provides a fun playground and can also be very unforgiving. It only takes a few minutes to drown. There are many communities that do not have pools, quality instructors, or a curriculum to follow. There are few adult swim classes to improve your skills.

As a pro with expert credentials and experience I can assure you quality instruction to learn how to swim correctly the first time, and not have to unlearn bad habits that create your inefficient and exhausting movements.

You have the ability to teach yourself many skills, but <u>you</u> have to take action. You cannot learn what you do not start. Home hardware and improvement stores depend on your ability to view, read, and follow their simple step-by-step directions to learn how and complete projects. In school you had to read the book and take notes to learn new information, process it, and take action.

If you can play catch with your kids, you can teach them basic swimming skills at home to start without a pool. Videos and pictures in a sequence along with specific how to instructions using visual, verbal, and kinesthetic feeling cues easily teach you how. The sequential system and mastery of each step along with four other teaching methods are my keys to getting fast results.

National and local swim programs generally do not spend time teaching water safety concerns outside of a clear, heated pool. When you overestimate your swimming and floating ability, you get fooled in unfamiliar water environments. You get caught in undertows, rip currents, or river currents, and do not use caution around marine life because you do not know what to do.

Many adults, despite having learned how to swim in an instructional program, never master how to do their breathing to swim continuously without building up an oxygen debt and stopping in the pool. You may be one who swims inefficiently with your head out of water the whole time to quickly exhaust your muscles and breathing. Floating skills are essential when you cannot stand up on the bottom and need to rest.

Learning to swim with your breathing efficiently helps you maintain your active lifestyle longer. When you learn to float you can swim better, and increase your effort to improve your cardio-vascular fitness.

The national problem is that 60% of adults cannot swim 20 feet to save their life. You either never learned how to swim or swim so poorly you fear not making it in the deep end of the pool trying to do fitness laps.

Fear of drowning is a terrible phobia. Overprotective parents can unknowingly condition this behavior, and unless you break the cycle you could be instilling the same fears in your children!

Fear robs you of all the potential water borne recreation you could be enjoying with your family and friends. <u>YOU</u> could be having more fun, too, by taking action to learn how to teach yourself now with all the simple easy-

17

to-master steps in this book. You will learn all about hypothermia, wave action, currents, floating and physics principles, propulsion, resistance, and the psychology of how we learn skills. You have the opportunity to learn how to swim several different strokes and resting skills if you get into trouble, and be more confident in and around water.

This week, by chance, I spoke with Doug who said he had just turned 40 but did not know how to swim. His kids knew how, but he would sit in the boat while they had fun in the water. This is more common than you may know.

Several years ago on a hot night I went to swim laps at the park district pool in Apple Valley, MN, but had to give up because they had not set up lap lanes. As I stood at the wall in the pool next to a middle-aged couple, their son swam in and out like a fish. She said to her husband, "I wish I could swim like that."

I knew then why I was directed to the pool that night. I put my goggles up on my forehead and politely told her I was a swim pro, and could teach her how. In 20 minutes she was able to swim 15 feet out to her husband. In another 20 minutes we worked on the pool side to show her simple drills she could use to teach herself how to condition rhythmical breathing to swim continuously non-stop.

The point of these two stories is all about readiness. You can safely walk across the street to get to the other side when you look both ways. When you take that action, you increase your confidence with the knowledge YOU put in your brain that it was safe to cross.

Learning to swim is a lot like that. **YOU have to take action to decide to learn.** That is your first step. When you accomplish the first step, this leads to the next simple step in a progressive sequence of steps you can master because **YOU CAN DO** each step. Each step rewards you enough to want to continue learning more and more until you become more confident and skilled. This is why my illustrated book has over 300 mini steps using my 6 unique teaching methods and specific cues that are different from any other program to teach you how to teach yourself.

The rules are simple. YOU cannot advance to the next step until you master that step. If you think you already know how to swim, then it should be no problem for you to start with step one and do each perfectly! In no time you will be where you think you wanted to be when you started in my program. If you violate this rule, then be prepared to hold yourself accountable when you are not satisfied with your performance.

I do not recommend you start on any higher step than #1. Your brain needs to be conditioned or retooled to do these fundamental motor patterns correctly. There is a reason why my sequence of steps works!

YOU may find a missing link in your knowledge and skills that will improve your performance when other strategies and tips you have tried in the past have not worked well. If you choose to start on a higher step, and find you cannot do that step very well you must agree to drop down to the previous step or steps until you can prove to yourself that you can do those steps well. Keep stepping back until you find your weak link that causes you to be inefficient.

My first week of practice at Indiana University, my coach, Doc Counsilman (who became the World's Greatest Swimming Coach), directed all of us including our All-American's and World Record Holders to do push offs and glides, and dives off the blocks for distance.

Back in 1961 Doc was a fat guy, but he could dive in off the block and on one breath glide the whole lap or 75'. I don't know what the other guys were thinking, but I thought, "Wow. If this fat guy can do this, I can, too!" I don't think I made it halfway on my first few attempts, but I did keep improving until I could make it about 65 feet.

The point of this is that you learn the most about laminar flow from your skin and other sense organs to reduce resistance when you are barely moving. You learn how to stretch and streamline your body to reduce drag resistance. Depending on the length of your race and your physical conditioning, you lose great amounts of time when you become tired and create more resistance perhaps the last 10% of your race.

Conditioning through workouts can help you acquire the optimum pace to conserve energy, and not degrade speed at the end of your race. But if you never took time to learn how to use the water and the physics of buoyancy and laminar flow, none of this will matter. If this practice to learn such a fundamental skill was good for Doc and World Record Holders, why do you think you are any different?

This illustrated book and optional hours of step-by-step instructional videos explain how to overcome your fears and relax so you can float in a variety of ways. I have six unique teaching methods no other instructor uses to communicate clear, concise messages you can process and physically perform. I also take time to explain numerous water safety concerns so that once you learn how to swim and get out of the pool into another environment you will know what to expect and be prepared.

An ounce of prevention is still worth a pound of cure especially when a human life is involved.

You will also learn basic physics principles like Newton's Three Laws of Motion, Bernoulli's Principle, and the psychology of learning to condition new motor behaviors to make them permanent. Then I will show you how to apply your knowledge to swimming correctly and efficiently to conserve your energy by being able to process your own feedback wearing goggles.

Swimming efficiency is simply based on reducing resistance to the body moving through water while increasing the surface area and force involved with propulsion over a longer range of motion.

I frequently refer to **DPS or distance per stroke. It is far better to take a few good strokes than a lot of fast poor ones** and go nowhere while expending 10 times the energy to use up your oxygen and get into trouble.

If you or someone you know look like you are climbing out of the water, you are not using the physics force of buoyancy to assist you. Have you ever observed a beach ball full of air skimming over the water in a slight breeze? Don't even think of going after it or an air mattress or inner tube. Let someone in a power boat go retrieve it. When swimming, always keep a reserve supply of air to inflate your lungs at all times.

Children grossly overestimate their swimming ability and easily get into trouble outside of a pool environment. They also regularly tell their parents they know how to swim, and their parents believe them!

I know how to paint, but I am not Van Gogh or Picasso. Swimming skills have this same variability. Just because you can swim 10-20 feet does not make you a good safe swimmer in different environments.

All park district pools have lifeguards that make kids and adults pass a swim test to go into the deep end. That test is usually 50 yards or two lengths in a 25 yard pool. What or how kids swim that test only matters if they can make it without stopping. Unless they are on a swim team, 99% of them swim with their head completely out of the water switching back and forth to breath.

How long could you last swimming so inefficiently 2, 5, or 10 minutes? If YOU swim like that because you never learned how to swim with your breathing, YOU have a problem.

Whether it is <u>YOU</u> or your children or your grandchildren, you must be sure of your swimming skills to be efficient. **IT IS NOT GOOD ENOUGH SIMPLY TO SAY YOU ALREADY KNOW HOW TO SWIM.**

The true test of your swimming ability is to take a walk in the park - only you will use the pool to swim some distance <u>NON-STOP</u>. If you can relax and float, take long slow strokes, exhale in the water 20% of your air like you do when walking, and inhale 20% back in to supply enough oxygen to your working muscles to keep going, then you will have passed the critical test.

The problem is that many instructors want you to start swimming right away. They breeze through the floating skills you still need to master to relax and not tense up. They unconsciously create the mindset that if you don't rapidly move your arms and legs you will sink.

Stiff muscles use up your oxygen quickly. To get more oxygen you lift up your head, but this drops your hips and legs down. Now you're swimming like a barge instead of skimming like a water ski. This inefficiency creates more demand for air to quickly exhaust you and put you in trouble.

Another great problem is that as a parent you falsely assume that if your child is taking swim lessons he will learn how to swim and be safe. You probably give more thought to choosing your dentist, and certainly would like to know if your surgeon is board certified and performed more than a few surgeries successfully.

You probably also assume that the instructional methods and curriculum are sound because they are the Red Cross or YMCA - huge national programs. But this does not mean the instructors have been taught how to teach correctly by experienced swimming professional teachers like me using advanced teaching methods and cues. My guess is that less than 1% of all instructors have even heard of Bernoulli's Principle and how to apply this principle to their swimming instruction.

The problem with some national and local programs is that they are out-of-date because they have not changed their standardized teaching methods or cues to get better predictable results. There is no quality control. High school aged kids make up the bulk of the summer instructor group, and they are lucky if they have already had physics to apply those principles in their teaching.

Requiring a standard to pass on to another level in a program is a good idea. But to require all the instructors to teach the same outdated methods and cues is like asking a college professor to teach the same way for 20-30 years, and how would that benefit those students?

Large or small franchised programs provide no guarantee of experienced instructors. In fact, many instructors have only been teaching for a few years or months, and are not competitive swimmers to know kinesthetic "feeling" cues from advanced personal skills they can demonstrate. How can you provide the correct cue to learn if you have never felt the result?

When I taught my high school instructors who would teach our local grade school children, I would not allow them to wear long-sleeved sweatshirts on the deck. You cannot demonstrate the visual arm position to develop the correct motor pattern if you cover up the arm. It is how the brain learns, but instructors violate this every day.

To summarize:

1. Don't overestimate your swimming ability.
2. Tell your kids, "Don't tell me you know how until you can show me all the basic skills."
3. Choose your swim program and instructor(s) wisely to know their credentials and experience.
4. Ask to see their curriculum or teaching lesson plans.
5. Be able to pass the "Walk in the park" test.

About Teaching Yourself

Home improvement companies like Home Depot, Lowe's, and Menard's have done well marketing the idea that with the right tools and instructions you can make simple and some complex repairs or construct things for your home. Their "how-to" guides take you through a sequence of steps. This is like the swing set instructions you used to put that together. Each step is so simple it only involves placing nut B on bolt A.

When you went to school, your teacher created verbal images, showed examples, demonstrated some skills to give you a visual idea of what to copy, and then verbally provided specific instructions how to perform parts or segments in a sequence. In some cases you took notes to recall how to do the sequence of events. Other times, you had to immediately translate what you were told - all the cues - into a physical action.

What I do is the same only instead of a teacher providing immediate feedback about how close you came to correctly performing that skill step, I teach you how to judge your own feedback. You will use goggles, your ears, eyes, and feeling receptors in your hands and forearms and other body parts to feel the water pressure and assess your movement efficiency.

If you are an adult who never learned how to be relaxed and efficient, it's hard to find an adult swim class. This book and video package fills that gap. You may also live in a part of the country that does not have pools - indoor or outdoor. You may have to use a back yard above ground pool, you cannot push off the side or swim more than 10-15 feet, but you can learn a lot.

I have lived in parts of the US where the "swimmin' hole" was a deeper part of the local creek. Rivers, lakes, and oceans can be dangerous places to learn because they have swift currents and wave action. The water is not as clear as a pool to provide good feedback on how you should be performing the skills underwater as shown in the videos and book picture sequence. With any coordination your brain can process the information like when you were in school to teach yourself to swim like a pro.

You can't finish learning how until you start to take action. Follow the steps and practice them all until mastery and you will be pleased with your results.

I find that many people have the mindset that if they don't move their arms and legs they will sink. They also think that if they rapidly move their hands and arms through the water that they are swimming better!

Efficient swimming is based on two simple principles: 1) You want to float and **decrease resistance** to your forward progress created by any body part outside an imaginary midline or plane cutting through your body like a spindle or rod to roll about on that axis, and 2) **Increase propulsion** of the surface area and lengthen the range of motion of that force application.

Imagine a water ski rope stretched out underneath you. As you take a freestyle stroke you reach out in front of you in the midline plane and grab hold of the rope. Then you pull yourself forward the first half, and push yourself forward the second half of each stroke to move over the top of the water.

If your body is not moving forward with little effort because you are floating, then you are not using proper mechanics to hold on to the water. **You have to learn to feel the water pressure on your hand and forearm with each stroke** as if you were reaching over a barrel. If your hand and arm are slipping by, then you are like a car spinning your wheels on ice.

**It is far better to take a few good long strokes than to take
a lot of short fast poor ones.**

Ch. 2   Need for water safety knowledge and skills

1. DROWNING STATISTICS

The Centers for Disease Control and Prevention in Atlanta Georgia report credible statistics each year. As stated before, ten people drown each day in the United States. For children ages 1 to 4 drowning is the leading cause of death. Children gain easy access to plastic, inflatable, and above ground backyard pools that are not fenced in. By race, African-Americans and Hispanics experience a much higher unintentional drowning rate than Caucasians.

Males account for 80% of unintentional drowning victims. The statistic that struck me the most was that children 14 and younger grossly overestimate their swimming ability, and unintentional drowning is the second leading cause of death in this group. This means you cannot assume your children know how when they tell you they know how to swim. Get them to demonstrate their swimming and water safety skills and compare that skill against a known standard that you have observed from pictures in this book or the videos available on my website: www.LearnToSwimProgram.com/Swim-Tips.

Kids get familiar with swimming in their local clear heated pool. Most swimming programs do not teach more than pool safety concerns to learn what to avoid or do in other aquatic environments. This leads to serious problems when parents or grandparents take them on vacations to the ocean, large lakes, fast-moving streams, and on boating excursions.

Knowledge and understanding the forces of water in wave action, currents, undertows, and hypothermia prevent panic and unintentional drowning. However, few swimming instructional programs take the time to explain what can be expected in other aquatic environments. Every grade school and high school, with or without a pool, needs one physical education class period set aside in the curriculum to learn about other aquatic environments.

Many parents use lifeguards as kid-sitters while they relax and don't watch their kids. You must assume personal responsibility for your swimming safety, and that of your immediate family and friends. While lifeguard training has improved immensely over the last 10 years, there are elements that lifeguards have no control over that can cause drowning such as stepping off piers or swimming in unmarked areas with breakwaters, rocks, wave action, currents, etc.

There are common factors that create accidents in and on the water. The most obvious is the use of alcohol while operating a boat, jet-ski, or other motorized equipment. In 9 out of 10 boating accidents the person who drowned was not wearing a life preserver. For every drowning there are four near drowning victims. In many of those cases the brain is deprived of oxygen that can cause serious brain injury for the rest of one's life.

When your children say they know how to swim, do not assume they can swim any kind of distance or have floating skills that enable them to be relaxed and comfortable to rest in other kinds of water environments.

Many of the teaching methods and cues in swimming have not changed or been modified much in the last 50 years.

Children have an 88% higher chance of surviving an aquatic accident when they know how to swim. There is no other sport you can learn that has the potential to save your life.

I would like to think that all of the national and local swimming instructional programs provide a good basis for efficient swimming for the rest of your life. But until all programs are fully capable of teaching you how to master all the necessary skills to be efficient for the rest of your life, take the time to master each step to become totally proficient.

2. KIDS OVERESTIMATE THEIR SWIMMING ABILITY

As was previously reported by the Centers for Disease Control in Atlanta, children 14 and under grossly overestimate their swimming ability. Once a child feels like he can swim a short distance to qualify to swim in the deep end and go off the diving boards, he feels safe. At that young age they have energy to burn, but that does not mean they have mastered the fine art of swimming efficiently. Consequently, when they grow up to be adults and want to swim out to the raft, they may think of themselves as still being 12 years old, but they are still unskilled and easily get into trouble without knowing resting skills to recover well enough to save their own lives.

As a parent or grandparent, you want to make sure that all your children can demonstrate efficient swimming skills for a variety of strokes for a variety of situations that can be expected when they leave the swimming pool. Once you have observed their proficient skills, ask them to start teaching their friends those skills. Challenge each and every one to continue learning to be efficient in the water.

3. UNDERSTANDING PANIC

When you are not familiar with what to expect and are unskilled to control a life threatening situation, you can easily go into panic mode. In a state of panic your brain literally shuts down its thinking capacity and subconsciously shifts toward self-preservation. You are not conditioned to know that you should take a large breath and hold it in until you float to the top. Then you can level off with less resistance to swim to safety.

What typically happens when people are tossed into the water either out of a boat or off a pier, they begin to struggle immediately because they do not put their heads and chests down which would raise their legs and hips up. Victims exhale but do not inhale to inflate their lungs to float. When they arch their heads up above water to breathe, their hips and legs go down vertically preventing forward swimming.

Panic victims will reflexively exhale their air as their diaphragm breathing muscle tenses up. Then they pant like a dog, but do not forcefully inhale enough to inflate their lungs to help them float. They quickly become exhausted and sink.

One of the critical steps that I condition is to take an immediate breath and hold it until your body floats to the surface keeping your head down to raise up your hips and legs. Once you are leveled off you can begin swimming to safety with less effort.

In cold water, parkas and heavy outer wraps absorb water to weigh you down like a wet sponge. You must wear a life preserver to stay afloat. If your lungs do not displace enough water to buoy you up like a balloon, you become a dead weight and sink after your muscles become rigid and exhausted from all the adrenaline. This only takes a few minutes.

Always remember that, **"An ounce of prevention is worth a pound of cure."**

The best prevention is learning how to swim efficiently with more skills, knowledge, and understanding of other environments besides your local heated pool.

Change your mindset from feeling like you have to rapidly move your arms and legs or you will sink. Instead, think about fully inflating your lungs and floating on top of the water. Then level off to use your arms to pull and push your body on top of the water with a mild kick to keep your legs up. Floating is key to your efficient success in swimming, and you will spend time learning to improve your floating skills.

With floating skills you can swim in almost any kind of environment with the knowledge that you will not sink and can go with the flow wherever that water takes you in a wave, stream, or a current of any kind.

4. LEARNING HOW TO IMPROVE YOUR SKILLS

The easiest way to determine if you are improving is if you are moving when you take strokes in the water. If you are taking lots of strokes and not moving, you would have to assume that you are not stroking correctly and are inefficient. This is your personal feedback.

I teach you first response conditioning to take a breath and hold it until you can level off and start stroking. Once you are floating, it takes little or no effort to pull your body over the water unless you are vertical or perpendicular to the water surface. Then you will expend lots of your energy and air and go nowhere but down.

By learning in small segments, you will feel rewarded and motivated to continue learning that next new step having mastered the one before it. Your job is to feel more consciously aware of your improvement. You can do this by pushing off and gliding across the pool for a set distance, and try to improve upon that distance each time you do a push off. The idea is to float relaxed and swim effortlessly across the pool.

The thumbnail photographs provide a standard to judge how well you are performing each of the steps. When you're able to more closely copy the sequence pictures in the book you should feel success, and transfer the same identical elements to the pool starting in the shallow end to eventually swim in the deep end with the same skills.

5. THE RESPONSIBILITY FOR YOUR PERSONAL SAFETY IS NOT YOUR LIFEGUARD'S

A swimming pool or beach may post lifeguards, but this does not relieve you of your personal responsibility to practice safe swimming. You must practice your skills to feel comfortable in the environment you are going to swim.

Cold water can bring on hypothermia faster than you might think. It can take your breath away, and cause your muscles to rapidly tighten up and lead to exhaustion in a few minutes. In water less than 50 degrees you may have less than an hour before you pass out and drown. In colder climes, it's wise to check the weather report and the boat you might board before you venture on to cold water. That fish is not worth your life.

6. YOU ARE NEVER TOO OLD OR TOO YOUNG TO LEARN HOW TO BE SAFE FOR FITNESS AND RECREATION

Swimming is a learnable skill for almost everyone. However, you must have an open mind to process the cues, and have the flexibility in your muscles and joints to perform the proper movements. Efficient swimming does require some flexibility. But you can also make several adaptations to decrease resistance and increase propulsion just as well.

Swimming is a great fitness activity because water has more resistance than air and reduces the effect of gravity on your joints. But if you fear not being able to make it to the deep end, you may not prefer swimming to maintain your cardiovascular fitness. My aim is to teach you efficient techniques you can easily learn and apply now so that you can maintain your active lifestyle in to your 80's. When you master these skills, teach others to join you in workouts, and join the US Masters Swimming organization www.USMS.org to gain valuable coaching tips, and promote "Swimming Saves Lives" on their website.

For recreation, water has endless possibilities. Besides boating you have lap swimming, water skiing, inner tubing, rafting, sailing, kayaking, canoeing, fishing, surfing, body-surfing, windsurfing, snorkeling, SCUBA diving, skurfing, and kite boarding to name a few various types of water recreation. I have done almost all of these. These kinds of activities are what keep you young and fit for many years to come.

A great resource is www.NDPA.org – The National Drowning Prevention Alliance. On their website you can find tips to prevent drowning, safety awareness campaigns, and a list of quality swimming schools. To get your child involved in competitive swimming go to www.USASwimming.org to find a local team.

Go to http://www.USSwimSchools.org to locate a quality swim school in your area.

You can email me: drpete@LearnToSwimProgram.com with questions or use www.LearnToSwimProgram.com/Contact-Form

You can get my current address and office telephone number from my website:

www.LearnToSwimProgram.com

You can subscribe, friend, or leave a comment, like or share suggestions for improvement

http://bit.ly/FaceBook-LearnToSwimProgram

http://bit.ly/YouTube-LearnToSwimProgram

https://www.linkedin.com/in/drpeteandersen

http://www.Twitter.com/drpeteandersen

For continuous improvement and coaching help, enroll today in my monthly Q&A Blue Ribbon Group program on my website.

http://www.LearnToSwimProgram.com/Membership

Normally it's $27 and valued over $150 in lessons!

Here's what you get each month:

1. Two 50-60 minute instructional/coaching webinars followed by your questions you can ask ahead of time so if you cannot attend, you'll hear your answers on the replays

2. Each week a new Chapter video from the curriculum in sequence to cover all the strokes plus water safety.

BONUS DISCOUNT

For getting my book(s) and becoming a part of my family of friends and Ambassadors of Swimming, I reward you with a lower enrollment fee of only $17 per month.

YOU MUST USE THIS DISCOUNT CODE AT CHECKOUT

SWIMFAST

Ch. 3   Personal guarantee and disclaimer

7.   MY PERSONAL GUARANTEE AND DISCLAIMER

If you follow my prescribed sequence of steps and practice enough to master each step, you will learn how to swim. For the videos you have 30 days unconditional guarantee from the date of shipment. If you are not committed to learning and practicing, then I would prefer you defer your investment or gift someone in need.

This guarantee is null and void if you are physically and mentally unable to read and/or perform any or several of the skills due to obesity, joint flexibility, injury, deformity, muscle weakness, sprains or strains, or mental condition.

I am not a medical doctor prescribing medical advice. I have a Ph.D. in how we learn motor skills based on psychological principles. From my personal experience, I may explain how I avoid swimmer's ear and fungus infections simply by drying out the outer ear canal with toilet paper on my little finger. This personal practice is not dispensing medical advice.

What you choose to take from this book is at your own direction. What knowledge and skills you choose to share with other people is your right, and I encourage you to help save more lives.

8.   THANK YOU FOR TAKING ACTION

It's never too late to improve your lifelong swimming skills. It's easy to believe that unintentional drowning and near drowning happens to the other person.   But if you watch the news, you probably have learned about someone in your area who has drowned in the last two years.

I want you to be completely satisfied with the content of this book and/or the videos.   You can search on Amazon and find that there is no instructional swimming video series available. There are competitive coaching technique videos which is entirely different from my instructional series.

This book benefits the active lifestyle, parent and grandparent, competitive Masters, Senior Olympians, and triathletes as well as the non-swimmer or novice and inefficient.   Instructors benefit by learning new teaching methods and cues that get fast results and save more lives.

You purchased this book to improve your swimming efficiency. You will need to continue to take action to learn each and every step in the sequence for this to be effective for you. As you master each small step you will feel a sense of accomplishment and be motivated and challenged to learn more in the next step. Build your support network by telling your family and friends what you know and are doing.

I have coached All-Americans and know that coaches like to tweak the fine points, but sometimes neglect the imbedded fundamental motor patterns that cause the confusion and prevent improvement in efficient technique to swim farther and faster. Not all great coaches are also great teachers. The psychology of learning in my six teaching methods plays a greater role than the simple application of physics principles.

Use your feeling of reward to build your confidence and motivation to learn all that you can from each of these steps. Being able to say that you know how to swim is not enough. You must also be able to say with clarity that you are comfortable swimming other strokes and in all kinds of aquatic environments by knowing the action and force of water.

Ch. 4   Your personal benefits teaching yourself

9. VALUE COMPARISON TO TEN ½ HOUR PRIVATE LESSONS AT $30 PER ½ HOUR

If you were to take ten ½ hour private lessons from a swimming instructor, he would charge you a minimum of $20-30 per ½ hour. This would include time spent for him to explain and demonstrate a specific skill, and your time practicing to master that skill. At the end of your 5 hours of instruction, you would probably know how to swim one stroke – freestyle, but perhaps not yet with efficient breathing technique.

Otherwise, why do so many adults and kids (except those on swim teams) still swim with their heads out of water at the local pools? You may be exposed to other strokes such as backstroke, breaststroke, and elementary backstroke, but not have time to master them without additional lessons. You may have never been taught excellent floating and resting skills to apply in open water when in trouble. But I will teach you these fundamental safety skills now if you will only take action to learn them.

A parent with two kids or more has to keep paying for multiple lessons for all the kids when one investment can provide all the fundamentals you will need for all of them as well as your friends and other relatives.

I also take time to teach you the equivalent of at least one lesson on water safety concerns outside of a clear heated swimming pool. In my experience, I have found that many instructors do not get in the water, and are not able to demonstrate the skills as they should. You will see a sequence of thumbnail pictures demonstrating how to do each skill. I've not found many instructors who spend time teaching you about water safety concerns outside of the pool. One result is that people get into trouble in unfamiliar environments on vacation.

Along with the visual picture sequence you'll be given a detailed verbal explanation of how to perform each skill that includes kinesthetic or feeling cues. These cues in combination prove highly resistant to forgetting and condition you to master each skill faster.

For a small investment, this paperback book provides a lifelong resource benefit you can take to the pool to review and compare to your skills. You also have the opportunity to invest in several hours of a complete DVD video instructional curriculum of easy-to-master steps. Ordinary lessons require repetitive payments. You have to decide their value based on results for a return on your investment. Good experienced instructors do make a difference, but there are not enough of them in all parts of the world.

In lessons, most of your time is spent listening to your instructor explain what I show you how to teach yourself with personal feedback cues. The video series provides a resource that you can continually refer to and share with all of your family and friends, and maybe split the investment to learn at your own pace and not feel rushed to get your money's worth.

As your body composition ages losing strength and flexibility, or if you suffer from a temporary injury or setback, sometimes those lessons you took several months ago are forgotten. But with the videos and the sequence pictures in the book, you can review, learn, and practice your skills on your own time.

10. WHY AND HOW _YOU_ CAN TEACH YOURSELF THE RIGHT WAY

The benefit of illustrated pages is like putting together a swing set in your backyard. Manufacturers provide you with a visual step-by-step sequence for you to put the swing set together with just a few basic tools. You must read the pages, follow the specific instructions in sequence, and then apply and process that information until you get it right.

Read the pages and steps in this book to follow the step-by-step sequence. You may mistakenly think that you can do any of these skills and skip around them. Well, prove it to yourself that you can. It will only take you a minute if you already know how. **The sequence is the key to mastery.** Each small step that you master in that skill makes it easier to learn, reward, and master the next step and so on to continue learning more advanced skills.

If you are not learning to improve today, it is because you stopped learning before mastery of key steps like coordinated breathing to swim freestyle continuously.

If you are a competitive swimmer and not getting any faster, you may not have mastered the spatial awareness to provide good body position and streamlining to reduce resistance.

I assume that you can process visual, verbal, and kinesthetic cues and have enough joint flexibility to perform each fundamental skill. If you are physically unable to perform a specific skill, you will need to make an adjustment to your stroke so that you can still perform that skill reasonably well. Your focus will still be on floating, streamlining, and propulsion.

I take complex skills and break them down into several sub routines or smaller parts that you can easily master with a little practice. Then I chain the sub routines together to perform the entire actual skill. This is why you must follow the specific sequence that I suggest for you to learn faster and be able to teach others.

11. VISUAL DEMONSTATIONS, FEELING CUES, VERBAL HOW-TO DO INSTRUCTIONS

The thumbnail sequence pictures show you how to perform what you are reading about feeling cues. More complex skills will have a set of sub skills or sub routines to learn in smaller steps. When you practice these sub skills in the water or wherever they may be such as at home in front of the dressing mirror or on your bed, pay close attention to the feeling cues that I suggest for you as well. Visualize your body and its position. Talk to yourself and self-correct if you are not in the position that is described in the words and pictures.

The human mind has a great ability to copy what it sees. Visualize in short term memory, and copy those skills by telling your body parts what to do. This is my teaching method known as mind control over your body parts.

This is not rocket science. When you were a child, you were able to toss a ball up into the air and catch it. Swimming is as simple as that. You get a general idea, and then once you go to the pool in the shallow end you perform exactly as you had imagined or visualized that skill in your mind.

12. FEEDBACK CUES TO SELF-CORRECT YOUR PERFORMANCE

My instructions give you specific feedback cues to help you self-correct your performance. Wearing goggles helps to see what you do underwater. Several of these cues require you to focus on what you are feeling when your hands and arms are entering the water. For example, if you don't feel water pressure on your hand and forearm when you begin to pull in the freestyle you are probably not pulling correctly. With your goggles you can see if you are reaching over a barrel or dropping your elbows to let your hand slip through the water after it enters.

Think of a car spinning its wheels on ice. The wheels turn very fast but the car does not move forward. Moving your arms and legs rapidly can be like that. You get the impression that you are swimming when you are not.

You float first and swim second. <u>Feel the water pressure on your hands and forearms to pull and push your body forward.</u> Look at the bottom to see if you are moving forward. It's better to conserve your energy and air supply by taking a few good strokes than a lot of fast poor ones.

Wearing goggles allows you to observe your swimming strokes above and below the water. In some steps you'll be standing in waist deep water to see your arm pattern as it performs each skill. You will condition the feeling in your hands and arms with what you see yourself doing compared to my demonstration. You can learn self-correction skills and not feel dependent on someone to tell you.

13. LIFETIME REFERENCE TOOL, NEVER OUT OF DATE

When you learn to teach yourself, it's easy to teach others and I hope you do to save more lives. The skills I teach you are more than what you might find in other books and programs at this time. The skills you master now will be as important 20 or 30 years from now for you, your children, and your grandchildren to master equally as well.

Using easy-to-master smaller sequential steps you can learn more swimming skills that many hours of private lessons do not provide. To be comfortable and skilled in the water you need to swim other strokes besides freestyle. To do a survival float or tread water, you must have floating skills and kick breaststroke. If you get into trouble and need to rest, you should know how to roll over on your back and float to recover your breath. This means you need to know backstroke floating and swimming skills, and sculling.

I see adults on vacation and nearly all of them swim with their heads and faces out of the water. They never learned to master their breathing as children in their swim program. Inefficient swimming leads to quick exhaustion that gets you in trouble, but this book illustrates how you can learn to teach yourself to master your breathing sequence and swim continuously like a walk in the park.

14. SHARE THE TOTAL CONTENT SEQUENCE WITH YOUR FAMILY AND FRIENDS

My hope is that when you learn to swim efficiently you will recall all of these specific cues, strategies, and teaching methods to teach others around you. This goes beyond your immediate family to your extended family and friends. My mission is to save lives. I need your help to learn these skills correctly and teach them to others. If you feel uncomfortable doing that then please offer to share the book (or videos) with others or recommend how they can invest in their own personal copy.

Knowledge of the forces of water and what to expect helps you avoid danger. Share your knowledge to keep others safe, too.

15. BONUS FEATURES – SAFETY AWARENESS, MORE ACTIVE LIFESTYLE

I spend a considerable amount of time educating you about other water safety concerns. However, this information will do you no good if you do not take the time to read these chapters. Water is everywhere. It's estimated that 65% of all recreation involves water.

If you live and play in and around water you must master these basic skills. Most of the awareness skills I will teach you are common sense. But you cannot assume that your children or your grandchildren have your common sense. Otherwise, for children ages 1 to 4 the leading cause of death would not be drowning.

My personal concern is that children 14 and under grossly overestimate their swimming ability. This can easily get them into trouble outside of a swimming pool. You may live next to the ocean, but this does not mean you are safety aware and efficient in your swimming technique. I have spoken to many people who live next to the ocean, and they are no more skilled than a person growing up in rural Kansas.

Parents, you cannot assume your children are as skilled as they think they are. You must have them frequently demonstrate their skills to you. Once they can demonstrate all of the skills in this book, you'll be more reasonably assured of their ability to protect themselves in and around the water.

I cover oceans, lakes, rivers, streams, and ponds to explain wave action, currents, marine life and hypothermia. I will also explain how to avoid electrical storms and electrocution, use proper equipment, and understand weights and measures to respect the power of moving water.

16. EASY TO UNDERSTAND CUES, IMPROVE EFFICIENCY, AND FITNESS

A cue is a stimulus to trigger a conditioned response. Over the years I have found that the cues used by several national programs are no longer effective to aid learning some skills. It is difficult for some of those national programs to change their curricula. This is a gross error of cause and effect. If you keep doing the same things and get the same poor results, then you must change what you do to get better results.

I provide you with specific cues that get fast results using my six unique teaching methods. You only have to focus on one body part at a time. My 50+ years with proven practical experience as a college All-American, coach of All-Americans, Masters World Record holder to correctly demonstrate these skills, and a doctorate in how we best learn motor skills, I have found that these cues work the best.

I use spatial awareness as the first of my six unique teaching methods to get you to focus on only one specific body part at a time, and know where that body part is in space. Take, for example, the pattern movement of your hand in and out of the water. If your mind is processing other kinds of sensory information, this will not help you to learn. I immobilize other body parts like having you stand still on the bottom of the pool for your brain to focus on only one arm or grasp the wall with both hands to blow large bubbles.

Once you build the specific motor pattern, you can transfer that habit to a pool much easier than if you were to try to couple that particular skill with other specific parts all at the same time. To your benefit, this is the value of my sequential system of steps. You get to learn at your own pace.

When you feel yourself in the water going farther faster with less effort, you become aware of your improvement to self-reward your skills in one-minute steps to keep you motivated. It is easy for you to monitor your performance. When you take a stroke, if your body is not moving forward for the amount of effort you have applied, you get immediate feedback that you may not be doing that skill efficiently. I teach you how to process your own feedback to learn self-correction skills so you can teach yourself to swim like a pro.

I provide you with an accurate visualization and verbal explanation with feeling cues to copy and compare to your performance. When you see accurate and effective movement for the amount of propulsion effort you apply, you feel rewarded and want to continue to learn more. This is why I use 300+ steps in my sequence so that you will feel frequently rewarded in one minute steps.

17. KNOW WHAT TO LOOK FOR IN AN INSTRUCTOR AND PROGRAM

As with any service whether you employ a contractor to lay tile in your home or build a deck the final outcome is called results. You can ask for references from people who have taken lessons from a private instructor to determine his effectiveness. You can ask for a copy of the curriculum to learn what you are paying for in what time frames. You can ask who the instructors are, how they are trained, and their experience. You can gauge this by their ages and whether or not they can perform the skills they are asking their pupils to perform.

Do not be fooled by the fact that a program provides certification. Paramedics never ask whether a drowning or near drowning victim was ever certified. It is hard to enforce quality control for any instructional system. This book and videos provide some basis to compare swimming instruction. If those "certified" cues are out-of-date, they are always out-of-date. Can the graduates swim with their breathing and know other strokes and survival skills?

Typically there are student instructors who are also lifeguards at your local pools. Hopefully, they are or have been on a swim team to accurately demonstrate and verbalize skills. But it's not likely that inexperienced student instructors will understand how to apply all the physics and psychology of learning principles found in my six teaching methods and numerous cues that get results until they read my book.

You can be assured that if your instructors get in the water they are more likely to be able to perform the skills they are asking their pupils to learn. Because a learner copies visual patterns it is imperative that the instructors do not wear bulky clothing such as sweatshirts, jackets, and sweatpants. The student will not be able to visualize the discrete curvature of the arm, the positioning of the legs in the kick, and the application of propulsion in the demonstration if the teacher is wearing bulky clothing.

As a rule, instructors will not produce a written curriculum with educational objectives, a detailed sequence of specific steps, or spend time teaching mastery of floating skills and all the water safety concerns for other environments as I do.

Many programs do not motivate their pupils to continue to learn more and more skills. Unfortunately, once parents and kids feel that they can swim a short distance, they think they are safe when they really are not. To be safe in and around water you must be able to swim continuously some distance and not just enough to swim in the deep end by passing that short 25 or 50 yard swimming test. It upsets me to see lifeguards pass students in this test who swim the entire distance with their head out of water never mastering their breathing technique.

These children grow up to be adults who make common mistakes going out to the raft thinking they can swim like they were 12 years old again. They may not master one of the most basic resting skills to simply roll over from your stomach to your back and float to recover your air because you've spent all of your energy in your poor efficient technique.

You may tend to think that you are safe because you can swim a short distance or have a life preserver handy, but the drowning statistics kept by the Centers for Disease Control in Atlanta, GA report that for 9 out of 10 boating deaths due to drowning, the individuals were not wearing a life preserver.

18. DON'T TELL ME; SHOW ME

The biggest mistake you can make is to assume that you know a skill before you perform that skill. Don't let your kids tell you or let you tell yourself that you know how to do something until you can actually do it. If you are that skilled, you can do each step in about one minute. If you find a step is too difficult you may need to go back to the previous step in the sequence, and spend more time to master that step and several of the steps prior to that one.

As you become more familiar with specific skills or tasks, your proficiency will gradually increase to help you learn the next step more easily. The value of taking the time to practice and master each step makes you feel rewarded for your accomplishments.

19. SEE CONSISTENT IMPROVEMENT AND CONFIDENCE; FEEL REWARDED

The strategy behind teaching you one-minute steps is the pleasure you feel when you master something and feel rewarded. With a very complex task like learning how to swim breaststroke you can easily be frustrated and give up. I break down this complex skill into several sub routines you can easily master one-at-a-time in a sequence I will chain together later. This process builds your confidence as you feel rewarded and motivated gaining mastery of that small step to keep learning.

It's a common psychological principle that you will want to repeat steps or skills when you feel rewarded, and avoid those when you feel failure. This is why I have broken down efficient swimming into multiple steps that you can take one at a time to improve your performance, and learn more than simply how to swim freestyle with your breathing.

After you learn how to swim freestyle efficiently, you will be challenged to learn other water safety skills and strokes to feel comfortable in other aquatic environments. I continue teaching more floating and resting skills, and then start with regular backstroke, floating, and resting skills followed by elementary backstroke, breaststroke, and water safety concerns.

All these skills together help you improve your confidence to enjoy other water activities, and maintain an active lifestyle for the rest of your life. Thus, the value is not in learning how to swim 25 or 50 yards, but in being able to swim other strokes and understand the action of water and its forces so that you are better prepared to avoid problems in and around water.

20. HOW TO USE EQUIPMENT - GOGGLES, KICKBOARD, ETC.

A good fitting pair of goggles with a silicone seal around your eyes is one of the most valuable pieces of swimming equipment you can buy. There are a number of online swim stores where you can purchase these kinds of goggles. What I recommend are the Speedo hydro-specs that you can buy from www.Kiefer.com or www.AllAmericanSwim.com.

Goggles let you see your stroke above and below the water so that you can master self-correcting skills as you compare my demonstration to your performance.

Many pools have kickboards but may not let you use theirs. They cost $8-$10 and kids jump, sit, or throw them around to break them. You can buy your own, put your name on it, and take it with you to the pool. Owning a kickboard provides you with upper body flotation to extend your arms and master the sequence and rhythm of kicking freestyle or breaststroke.

Hold the front or sides of your kickboard with your hands. Depending on how long your arms are, rest your elbows on the lower corners. You eliminate extra sensory information coming into your brain by stabilizing the board and extending your arms. You have enough room to place your face in the water between your arms and practice blowing big bubbles while you maintain a steady kick.

Ch. 5   What to think before you start to succeed

21. YOU CAN TEACH YOURSELF TO SWIM LIKE A PRO IN ONE-MINUTE STEPS

There are many places in the U.S. and world where you cannot find pools or highly trained swimming instructors. Even in populated places, there are few older experienced professionals to trust learning the right methods and cues to get faster, longer-lasting results that have the potential to save your life.

Few programs spend time teaching you water safety concerns outside of your clear heated swimming pool. Many do not openly market their programs or encourage patrons whom they see not swimming well to take lessons. Learning to swim continuously with your breathing is a sure way to improve your safety and family.

If you exclude adults who were once on a swim team, my estimate is that 90% of all adults have never mastered their breathing skills, despite taking lessons as children. The consequence is that they do not prefer to swim to maintain their active lifestyle and cardio vascular health benefits.

My marketing plan is to use social media to teach you how to swim at home without a pool. You can start to learn all the basic motor skills using a kitchen sink or wash basin, dressing mirror, mattress, and a bath tub. Then you can more easily transfer these identical skills to the shallow end of a pool. If you decide to take lessons, you'll get more value out of them. I envision elementary teachers teaching all of these home skills during physical education to help save more lives.

My illustrated book and videos are a constant resource. You will learn valuable feedback methods and cues to make self-corrections to all your swimming skills, and continue to learn and improve. The benefit is that if you are injured or cannot swim indoors during the winter months for a period of time, you can use these resources to regain your skills.

The oldest psychology of learning principle is that we want to repeat pleasure (our success) and avoid pain (our failure). I have broken down complex skills into simple easy-to-master steps in a curriculum sequence to increase your probability for success every step of the way. When you feel self-rewarded for learning a step, you are also encouraged to learn the next step with confidence.

When you pay for a private lesson, half of your time is spent learning from your instructor how to do a specific skill. Too often, your instructor may not get in the water to properly demonstrate that skill to get a visual idea as well as my photo sequence shows you. You pay for your performance/practice time. Whether you read my book and view the photo sequence or videos using methods and cues based on my 50+ years of teaching experience to know which get results, or listen to your instructor's explanation, you still have to process the information which is teaching yourself.

If your children take lessons, your charges multiply quickly when you could have taught these basics at home first. This is no different than teaching your children baseball, soccer, basketball, or golf skills they transfer to the game.

22. SHARE YOUR SUCCESSES WITH OTHERS

My book and video series is based on physics and psychology of learning principles. You benefit in getting the best methods and cues I have tested over 50 years of teaching which give you the best results and a constant valued resource to share with your family, relatives, friends, co-workers, and neighbors.

Do you want to get faster longer-lasting results learning to swim? Go to http://bit.ly/FaceBook-LearnToSwimProgram and subscribe to http://bit.ly/YouTube-LearnToSwimProgram

Learn about my six unique teaching methods, sequential steps, and numerous cues before you sign up for lessons. To get useful swim and safety tips plus how to choose a swimming instructor and program go to my websites www.LearnToSwimProgram.com & www.SwimVideoCoach.com

As each new swim season approaches, use your videos to review your personal skills, and water safety concerns outside of the pool where you may vacation with your family. For example, if you are planning to go to an ocean beach, review how to identify rip currents to avoid them.

You also get to learn at your own pace. You don't have to feel rushed because the hour meter is ticking off dollars in your private lesson. I teach you self-correction skills to gain valuable feedback observing your stroke mechanics above and below water using your goggles. Your body composition changes with aging or you can be injured to get out of swimming, and will need to correct some errors to remain efficient.

An instructor can only give you feedback about what you are performing at that moment in time and how to correct that specific mechanical error. YOU must still process that information and make the correction. Your instructor cannot do this for you. When you pass on what you have and know, you help save more lives. I am truly grateful for that.

23. YOU DID ALL THE WORK AND YOU GET ALL THE CREDIT

This is the 1200 seat two pool facility dedicated in 1957 where I learned how to teach swimming over 50 years ago. In March 2011, it was officially renamed the William Dobson Burton Aquatic Center at Evanston Township High School, Evanston Illinois to honor my coach. Dobbie passed away five months after the rededication of the pool, but what he taught us about life through competitive swimming lives on. My swimming instructor's instructor was our Director of Aquatics, John Terhune, who has long since passed away. Our progressive station system and curricula skills were copied by many high school programs at the time.

I will never forget riding home on the bus in late April my freshman year after teaching Saturday morning classes to our local grade school kids. We had to be assistants our first year. In our sophomore year after we proved our teaching skills, we could be primary instructors. On this Saturday morning, the primary instructor did not show up, and Mr. Terhune asked me if I was OK to take the whole class, and I did.

Going home on the bus I reviewed my morning and recalled a little boy who did what I instructed him to do. He swam (soloed) for the first time. Boy, I was hooked! From then on, I wanted to be a teacher and swimming coach because of my early experience with these two fine men.

Later, I would become close to two more fine men: Doc Counsilman and Hobie Billingsley the swimming and diving coaches at Indiana. Doc has passed away. This past July, I went over to Bloomington, Indiana to help all the divers celebrate Hobie's 85th birthday. And what a great motivational speaker he is today! I still get goose bumps listening to his stories about personal challenge.

The nice thing about swimming is that you have no one to blame for your lack of success if you learn to "pay the price" as coach would say. Later, I would recall this as a major paradigm shift in my life. **Quality of effort equates to quality of reward.**

YOU have to take action. I believe that if you have applied the sequence of steps and taken the time to master each one, you'll have quality results to show for your quality effort. Only you can judge the worth of your personal effort.

All I know is to keep trying to improve at whatever I choose to do. **In life I have viewed myself as an average person who tries to do a better than average job.** These skills and knowledge take time to master. There are no shortcuts to excellence.

The turtle was a plodder who beat the faster rabbit. Your values and priorities may be different. But **I can assure you that if you value being an efficient swimmer, you will also want to teach your children and friends what you know to pass on what I have taught you.**

My mission is to save lives while improving the quality of life through swimming activities. I want to thank you for whatever steps you have taken to help yourself and others.

You deserve all the credit.

24. YOUR CONFIDENCE IN THE WATER IS MUCH IMPROVED

Never take for granted any small accomplishment you achieve! You will feel a sense of accomplishment by achieving any small step. You feel rewarded, and this enhances your intrinsic motivation to keep improving to maintain the good feeling you have. This builds your confidence in the water. The more knowledge and understanding of the powerful forces of water to be efficient in swollen streams, currents, and waves, the more your overall safety awareness increases.

25. DON'T LET YOUR CHILDREN TELL YOU THEY CAN; HAVE THEM SHOW YOU WHAT THEY CAN DO!

Children and adults all the time tell me they already know how to swim. Then when I see them swim with their heads out of water the whole time, I understand why drowning is the second leading cause of death for children 14 and under. It's not a good idea for parents and grandparents to think that their children are safe at guarded pools, and beaches. Lifeguards have to watch over many people at the same time. This is a tedious job. Lifeguards are trained to recognize when a swimmer is getting into trouble, but they are not your kid-sitter. In a near drowning, there is often irreversible brain damage that can require care and expense for the rest of a life.

The best prevention is to learn to swim, and know about other aquatic environments. I said this earlier. **Learning to swim is the only sports skill that has the potential to save your life.**

It usually takes a minimum of five hours of lessons to learn how to do efficient freestyle with correct breathing. This book is written with illustrations for children five and older to understand and copy what they see and read to do. The video series offers more hours of instruction that includes swimming freestyle efficiently with breathing, elementary backstroke, regular backstroke, breaststroke, resting skills, and over 20 minutes of water safety concerns.

The water is fun, and it can also be unforgiving. When I teach lessons, I don't like to play games. I want you to acquire a respect for water because it is everywhere. You cannot survive without water, but it only takes a few minutes to suffocate you. You can learn to enjoy it and not fear it. Let the water work to float and relax you. Do not fight it; you cannot win against the power and weight of water.

If you or your kids cannot easily demonstrate a specific step, then you/they must go back to master the step before it. When you stay in the sequence it makes learning the next step much easier.

26. IT PAYS TO BE EFFICIENT – REDUCE RESISTANCE AND INCREASE PROPULSION; FLOATING IS THE KEY

When you sign up and pay money for lessons, instructors and pupils want to try to speed up the learning process to demonstrate benefits and value. They do not spend enough time mastering the basics of floating, and move right into kicking and stroking. Students acquire the mindset that if they don't move their arms and legs fast enough they will sink.

Time is money. Once you feel you can swim a short distance, you feel safe enough to quit taking lessons and save your money. You may think you will acquire more swimming skills naturally just by swimming. However, if you've not mastered all the skills such as breathing in your freestyle to feel comfortable and confident, you can easily panic in unfamiliar aquatic situations. This is why I spend a lot of time on water safety concerns to teach you in advance what to expect so you can avoid getting into trouble.

With my six unique teaching methods, you acquire a greater understanding of how and why you must swim a certain way. I don't make the rules. There are principles of physics and psychology that tell us why we have to perform specific skills one way over another, and how we can learn them easily with good cues that get faster results.

As you age, you lose strength and flexibility. It is imperative that you reduce resistance, and acquire floating principles you may not have mastered. Once you are floating and streamlined, it is much easier to apply propulsion to move you through the water efficiently. To be competitive, all you have to do is reduce resistance, and apply more force over a shorter period of time. When the race is over you get to rest. However, out in open water you are not racing, but you may be trying to survive by conserving your energy. Now it is imperative you know how to be efficient.

Once you learn efficient swimming principles, you can apply them to any situation to save your life, swim for fun, swim for conditioning and fitness, or to compete. And, you have an illustrated book as a resource to teach you how anytime you want.

27. WHEN YOU FIGHT THE WATER YOU LOSE EVERY TIME

In an earlier lesson, I pointed out that one cubic foot of water weighs 62.5 pounds, and contains 7.5 gallons each weighing 8.3 pounds. That 5 gallon bucket of water weighs 42 pounds. Thus, a small wave can weigh thousands of tons. A fast-moving stream could have a flow of hundreds of cubic feet per minute. Whether in a flood, knocked over by a wave into an undertow, or caught in a rip current that accounts for over 80% of beach rescues coming off the beach through that sandbar, you cannot fight the water and win.

Decide right now how floating correctly will help you to go with the flow perhaps sculling on your back with your feet forward to protect your body, and slowly sculling or swimming out of the main flow to safety.

Decide right now that you will learn more skills to feel more comfortable in the water. **By taking action now, the life you save may be your own.** Certainly by learning how to apply what you learn in these steps, you can help others as well.

28. DON'T ASSUME, BE IN CHARGE, PLAN AHEAD, AND PASS IT ON TO SAVE MORE LIVES

Don't ever assume you are safe 100% of the time. It's our human error to not improve our swimming skills and knowledge of the powerful forces of water. If you go out on someone else's boat, do your <u>own</u> inspection to know the engine is in good working order, the radio and antennae work, the fire extinguisher is charged, enough gas is in the tank to get out and back, the weather report is okay, and there are enough life preservers for everyone.

You can't be afraid to say something to your friends or family. Keeping silent about a water safety concern can prove dangerous. Whether your children like to hear your lectures or not, you have an obligation to maintain their safety by any means. Whenever I see an inefficient swimmer, I stop what I'm doing and offer my help. I missed a practice just this morning helping a 62 year old woman. People are always willing to learn how to improve their skills if what you say makes sense and gets results! In 20 minutes I had her swimming when at first she would not even put her face in the water.

When you pass on your knowledge, you provide a tremendous service to help save more lives. As a resource, this content can be shared by family, relatives, and friends for a long time. Parents who have multiple children can benefit by only having to make one investment, and teaching their own children all the fundamentals they need. Swimming is a natural process that anyone can learn, if he or she is willing to try and follow my sequence.

My mission is to save more lives worldwide with good instruction to teach you how to teach yourself efficiently with good results. People in rural and impoverished urban and suburban areas without pools and/or affordable quality instruction need help, too.

You can help me in two ways by joining my mission: 1) you can invest in this book and videos and teach others what you know and have learned, or gift them a copy and 2) become an affiliate to tell all your friends, family, and co-workers, and receive good commissions for recommending the content to others so they will also invest and help save more lives. Sign up for our affiliate program by going to:

www.LearnToSwimProgram.com/Affiliates

29. TAKE ALL THE POSITIVE ACTION STEPS TO LEARN AND PASS IT ON

The life you save may be your own. It's the dumb things in life that will kill you. Swimming skills without knowledge is dangerous because it breeds overconfidence.

An ounce of prevention is worth a pound of cure. Knowing what to expect and taking proper action is key to your survival. Children, mostly boys, 14 and under grossly overestimate their swimming ability, and get into trouble in water outside of a clear heated pool. Toddlers, ages 1-4, need to wear an approved life vest in and around water. The statistics show that they can improve their chances for survival from unintentional drowning by 88% if they are taught how to swim.

Small, portable backyard pools are not fenced in. Are your kids and grandkids safe or do you just assume they are because they take lessons? And don't forget hot tubs.

As adults we forget that we are not kids anymore. Heck, I can't catch a softball over my head like Willie Mays anymore. I have not practiced that skill for over 30 years! Is swimming like that for you? What do you really know about your kid's swimming skills? Maybe they should show you all the skills in the book and videos instead of telling you they can swim. If you find they are very inefficient and have no knowledge of currents or wave action, they may be a statistic waiting to happen.

Be in charge of your life, to warn those you love, and even complete strangers. Take the water seriously. It only takes a few minutes without air to pass out. Last time I checked, humans cannot breathe underwater without SCUBA gear because we don't have gills. Totally enclose your backyard pool or hot tub to secure entry from the house, too.

Teach your family how to swim using these videos as a group activity. You teach them about life and other things to be safer. Swimming skills are no different. When you follow my sequence you can quickly build their confidence to keep learning to master the next new skill. Or, would you rather they play video games?

Are several hours of viewing my swim videos worth your time when they may save your life or a loved one like a toddler? Instead of working on your tan this summer lying out next to the pool, get in the swim with your children, and learn to improve your skills. You'll have something to show for your summer.

Use your knowledge to pass on what you know to your children and grandchildren and friends. Hardly a day goes by that I do not take time out of a personal workout to help improve another person's swimming skills. **Word of mouth is a powerful tool unless you remain silent. Then you'll regret you did not take action. At the end of the day ask yourself, "Are you improving? If not, why not?"**

Ch. 6   Six new teaching methods get faster results

30. SPATIAL AWARENESS

Spatial awareness is your ability to know where all of your body parts are in space in any kind of movement. In the face float from your hands to your feet your entire body should be level on top of the water with your stomach sucked in. What typically happens is your feet and legs sink, but you think you are floating level. Or, you may separate your hands and feet and lose your streamlined body position. Or, lift your head up slightly too much to cause your legs to drop down.

This is where your spatial awareness comes into play. You must know from feedback in your feet that your legs are not floating on top of the water. You will know if your arms are spread apart because you will not feel your upper arms squeeze against your ears.

When it comes time to learning self-correction skills, I will ask you to observe your strokes above and below the water. After some observation you should be able to close your eyes and visualize a mental image in your mind of that same pattern you just observed with your eyes open. This will allow you to condition the feeling to gain more spatial awareness and perform each skill correctly.

31. MIND CONTROL OF BODY PARTS

Your mind controls your body, and your body carries it around. Your body does not control your mind. If you have to overcome your fears, constantly remind yourself that you have an adult brain. Use your brain to focus on imaging only the simple skill you are trying to learn as opposed to the fear of failure or drowning image that is preventing you from learning. This is why I start the sequence with very basic steps to help you overcome your fears by experiencing very small steps to develop your confidence, feel rewarded, and forget your fear.

You will learn to use your mind to focus on only one specific small step at a time to increase your odds for success, and build your confidence and ability to swim efficiently. But if you continue to dwell on the negative images that you cannot perform a skill, or learn it in a new and correct way, you most assuredly will not perform that skill – EVER.

We recently were fortunate to vacation with some of my children and grandchildren in Cancun, Mexico. I tried to help one of my daughters-in-law to change her breaststroke in the pool. Every cue I told her, she kept telling me that was not how she learned it. Her focus was on the old negative way, and would not allow her brain to learn a new more efficient way. Try not to create this problem for yourself.

32. SEQUENTIAL LEARNING

The key to my swimming instruction is the sequence of steps I ask you to master and focus on one at a time. It makes no sense to start you out on trying to master your breathing when you cannot properly float and move your arms to create movement. If you have fears to overcome, I start you out in your kitchen sink, bathtub, in front of a dressing mirror, and on a mattress at home.

Each step in the sequence is a stepping stone to the next step and so on. As you become more familiar with each step, the next step becomes easier to learn and perform. Then I chain together all the parts into a blended sequence of small skills to improve your timing and efficiency to do the whole stroke well.

33. MASTERY LEARNING

Any change you make to your current swimming pattern will seem uncomfortable to you. This is why you must turn each step into a familiar habit. Once you master that step it becomes more resistant to forgetting, and to make the next step easier to learn.

One common mistake that swimmers make is to think they already know how to perform a skill without actually mastering that skill. If you are as good as you think you are, then you should perform each step rapidly to perfection. However, if you are unable to copy the pictures and described skills, you must spend more time mastering that particular step.

If you have difficulty mastering a step, do not just stay on that one step but also go back to read, review, and self-test your ability to perform several of the skills steps prior to the one that you're working on. You may have worked past your proficiency and never truly mastered the previous steps.

34. FEEDBACK INFORMATION PROCESSING

Use your goggles to observe your swimming pattern above and below the water to learn how to self-correct your mechanical errors. The easiest feedback that you can process is your physical movement over the top of the water in relation to your energy expenditure. If you are not moving but using a lot of energy, then you are inefficient. Conversely, if you take little effort to move some distance, then you are efficient. Using up less energy and oxygen to swim continuously like a walk in the park is the ideal way to save your life, and a healthy way to improve your cardio vascular system.

When you learn my self-correction skills, you will not have to pay for lessons. But once you have learned what you can, you still have to practice what you learned. It becomes your responsibility to continue to learn what you can and not be satisfied with your current skill level.

All your basic motor patterns to swim efficiently can be started and practiced in the home without a pool using a kitchen sink, dressing mirror, bathtub, and mattress to teach yourself or your kids all the visual, verbal, and kinesthetic (feeling) cues.

When you read a book you must process the information that you are reading in order to learn verbal cues. Reading how to learn each skill is no different. Your goggles allow you to see visual cues in your pattern to compare to the ones shown and described in the book or on the videos. With practice you can copy the pattern and teach yourself the same as any instructor would demonstrate and describe to you. Only you get to take your time to learn at your own pace. In the visual and verbal cues are feeling or kinesthetic cues that associate to muscle tension and pressure receptors in your skin and joints.

35. TRANSFER OF IDENTICAL ELEMENTS

Very shortly you're going to be exposed to 30 specific skills you can easily learn to perform and practice without stress or fear in the comfort of your own home. You can also teach all of these skills to your children or your grandchildren, and as easily practice them on yourself, too. After you master each of these specific skills at home, you will transfer and repeat the same sequence of identical elements in the shallow end of the pool.

Similarly, you will practice standing in the shallow end of a pool to repeat all the specific sequence of steps and skills from home on dry land. Once mastered, you transfer the same identical elements to swimming a good distance on top of the water first in the shallow end. Then you transfer those identical elements to swimming a short distance across a corner in the deep end where the depth of the water makes no difference. By practicing small steps in sequence, your brain can learn new complex skills faster in routines that become habit.

Ch. 7   Fundamental home preparation steps to overcome your fears, build confidence and skills

You can learn a lot at home to save time and money on beginner lessons. Your brain must connect associational neurons to complete motor patterns. These take time to form and research evidence suggests this kind of home practice in between lessons also helps learning.

My point is why not do these first before you start to take lessons so that you can get more out of your paid lesson time? Or, why not teach yourself and your kids these fundamentals just like you teach them how to throw and catch a ball to develop those early skills?

If you are adult with an intense fear of drowning, then in the privacy of your home you can use your mind to overcome your fears without embarrassment. I have never learned of any adult that drowned in their kitchen sink. It's pretty tough to put your face in the water and want to inhale water. But if you can relax with both feet on the ground and put your face in the water for 10-20 seconds, you are well on your way to getting your mind to control your body parts to swim.

Ch. 8 Kitchen sink progression

36. FACE UNDERWATER - IN CUPPED HANDS

To overcome your fears and use your mind to control those fears about putting your head in the water, I use a kitchen sink so that you can lower just your face into the water, pinch your nose, and start to open your mouth. The water will not rush in, fill your lungs, and drown you. To my knowledge, no one has ever drowned in their kitchen sink. You have an adult brain, use it to sense and control your body parts.

To swim efficiently, you must learn to put your face in the water to float level on top of the water. Being relaxed and in control to float is highly important to your overall success. Now is the time to use your mind to control your body. With practice you will become familiar with putting your face in the water. Your intense fear will be replaced by a positive easy relaxed feeling that becomes your new behavior. This is mind control and behavioral conditioning.

Fill your kitchen sink about two thirds full and use your left hand to pinch your nose. Lower your face into your right hand right just below the water. While your face is submerged with your eyes, nose and mouth hold your breath counting for 10-20 seconds.

37. FINGER IN MOUTH

Repeat putting your face underwater and holding your breath. Take your underwater hand and use your index finger to insert into your open mouth and make a few circles.

As you focus on doing this keep in mind that the water is not rushing in to your lungs. An inverted glass submerged in water won't let the water rush in. You are making a better airlock in your nose by keeping your mouth open. This may be opposite to what major swim programs will tell you to do, but is exactly what every accomplished swimmer does – keeping their mouths open in the water.

Of course you will not exhale or inhale while you do this. You must also focus on the feeling of your eyes and nose in the water. This may seem uncomfortable to you at first, but mastering this simple skill will pay dividends for you in learning how to swim faster in the succeeding steps that will follow.

By keeping your mouth open and making a better airlock in your nose, you keep water from going up your nose to tickle those tiny hairs. If you close your mouth, those hairs get tickled and subconsciously tell your brain, "You idiot! Are you trying to drown me? Get my head above water." With that you pick your head up which drives your legs and hips down so you have to try to climb out of the water in a state of panic and go nowhere but to exhaustion.

The goal is to imagine yourself floating level keeping your head down to swim over the top of the water like a water ski.

38. SLOWLY EXHALE BUBBLES

Repeat putting your face back down in the water. With your mouth open blow bubbles and feel them float up from your mouth, around and over your cheeks. This is the start of your very first kinesthetic cue to feel an event. Subtle cues are important. For example, a wrong cue to exhale as if you were blowing out a candle encourages you to blow out tiny bubbles that take too much time.

Instead, you need to keep your mouth open and relaxed to blow out and feel large bubbles go up and over your cheeks. Then you can expel 20% of the air out of your lungs quickly, and not disrupt your breathing air back in. Your arms will swim and your head must turn to inhale at the appropriate time. But you cannot inhale until you exhale at least 20% of your air supply. When you cannot breathe in you have to stop swimming. This is a bad timing problem and why the next step is necessary.

39. EXHALE BIG BUBBLES OVER YOUR CHEEKS

To discriminate between blowing out slower smaller bubbles felt over your cheeks, open your mouth wider and slowly force out a large bubble or two to feel it go around and over your cheeks. Note how this feels entirely different than the small bubbles you just felt. When you practice this skill be sure your forehead is looking down at the bottom or you will blow bubbles up your nose.

By being relaxed and opening your mouth wider, you can expel at least 20% of your air in a much shorter period of time. Like walking in the park you must continually replace a portion of your air supply or you will build up an oxygen debt and have to stop walking or swimming as the case may be.

To regain your level body position after you have taken a breath, you have to put your forehead and face back down in the water looking at the bottom, and start to exhale immediately. This gives you more time to expel enough air to inhale new air when your head turns and clears the water surface as you roll your head and body up to breathe with every right arm stroke. You cannot wait to exhale when you start to turn your head; it's too late to get out enough air to breathe any amount back in and keep your body position level.

40. FACE UNDER THE SHOWER

By now you have plenty of experience rinsing soap out of your hair in the shower. Yet, you managed to inhale despite the cascade of water flowing around your face. Learning to swim with your breathing is no different. You get used to having your face in the water exhaling large bubbles, and as you rotate your face up to breathe you inhale a small breath. You don't suck in your air any harder than you would in the shower.

41. CHILD GUIDANCE - POUR RINSE WATER OVER YOUR CHILD'S HEAD

Prior to soaping your child's head up, take a plastic container and scoop clean water up from the tub to gently pour over his head a few times when he is sitting or on his stomach. Do this while your child is still very young and make it a fun activity.

Do not be alarmed if your child starts to cry or scream and does not like what you do. Simply continue to do this until he gets used to it. Make this as normal as getting in the tub. Infants are like golden retrievers, and easily sense your concerns. As the parent, you must not show any fear, but create the idea that this is a regular activity.

Ch. 9 Dressing mirror progression – eyes fixed on the mirror; no head movement

42. 40 TORPEDO STEP

Look directly at your eyes in a dressing mirror. If your eyes in the mirror start to move, it's not the mirror. Stand up straight with your feet planted firmly on the floor hip width apart. Imagine a rod fixed from your head to your toes about which you are going to roll your upper body around like a spindle while keeping your feet fixed. This step looks like a torpedo that can roll, but do not move your head or body from side to side or up and down out of the rod alignment.

This action will be most like when you actually swim on top of the water in a floating position. Now you have the opportunity out of the water to practice and build a motor pattern with specific skills steps and cues, and transfer these same identical elements to the shallow end of the pool when you are ready. By practicing at home you can develop these basic fundamentals to build your confidence, and learn to apply them easily when you get to a shallow pool.

Focus on keeping your eyes and head steady in the mirror so your brain will not process extra information. Roll each shoulder forward and backward so that one is in front of the other, and then reverse it to twist your upper body. Keep your head steady. There is no bobbing or weaving rolling about that imaginary rod to teach you how to stay on plane. Only your shoulders and upper torso do the twisting and rolling about your hips. Keep your feet in place so your brain can focus on the skill and not process extra information.

43. PROPELLER STEP

Lift your arms up straight from your sides so that they are completely level with your shoulders and opposite from one another. As you did in your torpedo step, I want you to rotate and place one shoulder and arm extended from that shoulder in front of the other with the other trailing directly opposite behind you. When you look in the mirror you can see that your trailing arm and shoulder are completely opposite from your forward arm and shoulder.

Focus on keeping your head steady and not allow your arm to catch up without the complete shoulder roll. You gain valuable feedback by making sure that your arms remain level with the tops of your shoulders. Practice slowly rotating each <u>arm and shoulder</u> opposite to one another back and forth several times.

44. SEESAW STEP

Your neck becomes the fulcrum and with your arms extended as you did in the propeller step, hold your lead arm and shoulder forward and rotate downward. At the same time as your lead arm and shoulder goes downward, like in a seesaw, your trailing shoulder, arm and hand must go upward to condition the feeling of this opposing motion. When the lead arm goes down, the trailing arm must lift up like a seesaw. This is what swimming will be like while floating. Keep your feet, head, and eyes fixed to focus all your attention on learning this step.

45. WINDMILL (FERRIS WHEEL) STEP

Start to imagine pulling yourself forward with your lead arm. Your trailing arm must start to lift up and come around to begin the next stroke and so on. This pattern looks like a windmill or carnival Ferris wheel. Keep your hands and arms opposite one another rotating your torso about the imaginary rod. Focus on your eyes in the mirror to keep your head steady. This gross motor action does not resemble good technique, but is necessary to gain a better feel for what you will transfer to floating in the pool.

46. PIVOT STEP

Like a basketball pivot step use your non-dominant foot (usually your left foot if you are right-handed). Fix that foot to the floor and step forward onto your right foot. You will learn to breathe on your dominant and stronger right arm. As you step forward onto your right foot, look into the mirror to see how you lift up your shoulder, arm and hand to extend your reach forward from your shoulder into the "hole." The "hole" is where both hands are together with fully extended arms to start your catch in the face float position you just performed in previous mattress steps. This action helps you increase your distance per stroke and be more efficient.

That imaginary rod going through your head down between your legs creates a midline plane you can observe in the mirror. Use your lead hand to rotate below your elbow, and follow that imaginary midline downward and backward. Pretend you are pulling and pushing yourself forward through the water while floating streamlined and level. At the same time roll and pivot step back to let your hand clear your hips and keep your hand following that imaginary midline.

As you roll your hips back to clear for your hand, be sure to follow through to push yourself forward like doing a push up before exiting your hand and arm out of the water. Emphasize rolling your shoulder back to make your forearm and hand exit with your palm flat. This makes it easier for your shoulder joint to recover your arms while swimming to avoid injury.

Note: If you are a competitive swimmer with shoulder joint problems, this is how to correct the mechanics that cause some of it.

47. SUMMARY REVIEW

You have now mastered five key home steps in front of your dressing mirror to transfer the same identical elements to the shallow end of the pool. The only difference will be to hold your breath and learn to float in the shallow end first before applying these steps. Or, if you prefer, you can repeat these exact same steps standing in the shallow end of the pool, and fixing your eyes on a wall or deck object.

It's important to master each of these specific steps to build your confidence and physical pattern to make them familiar skills. This becomes task familiarity. The more familiar you are with a task, the more confident and secure you will be. All these are learnable skills you can teach yourself and others.

48. CHILD GUIDANCE- KEEP THEIR HEAD STEADY AND BODY STANDING UP STRAIGHT WITH EYE CONTACT; INTRODUCE NEUTRAL POSITION

When you teach your child as a parent or grandparent insist that they do not fidget and keep their feet in place and focus their eyes in the mirror or on an object at the pool to keep their head steady. They need to learn how to rotate their body about that imaginary rod to be efficient. In order to learn these skills rapidly, the body must maintain its position to be efficient. If your body is moving all over the place, your brain must process all of that extra sensory information. This will not help you focus on a specific body part to learn that skill. Then all of their motor patterns can be observed, focused, and felt in the muscles correctly to behaviorally condition the routine.

Ch. 10   Bed and mattress progression

49. NEUTRAL POSITION

The mattress on your bed is a perfect place for you to stretch out your body or your child's body and learn what it feels like to be perfectly level. To be streamlined keep your upper arms pinned against your ears and legs together while lying on your stomach with your forehead resting on the mattress. Point your toes slightly so that your ankles rest completely flat on the mattress, and put one hand on top of the other.

This helps you acquire spatial awareness, a key teaching method I use. Then when you float in the pool holding your breath, you'll put your face down to keep your legs and feet on the surface. This is a learnable skill, and you can do it. Then when you get to a pool and do your floating steps, you can easily transfer this skill to do a push off and glide keeping your body perfectly level on top of the water in that face float position also known as your neutral position.

50. CHILD GUIDANCE- ANKLE BOUNCE AND FISHING ROD FLIP

Focus on the cue "tops of your ankles" that will beat and bounce on the mattress. Get a 1-2-1-2 rhythm count. Your ankles will not separate much if you imagine you are kicking both feet inside of a 5 gallon bucket. If you focus on the wrong cue to bend your knees, your ankles will lift up too high off the mattress to create drag resistance outside of the midline plane when swimming.

In the water your kick will not provide nearly as much propulsion as your arms. If you overly focus on your kick you will spend lots of energy when you should focus on your arms to provide you with more propulsion.

One way to help your child learn is to place two fingers above and below his knee with your thumb directly behind his calf. If he tries to lift the lower leg up too high from the knee, your thumb will provide a stop like you would use on a fishing rod and reel. You can also use your thumb to alternately press his calf back down to bounce the tops of his ankles on the mattress to teach the proper rhythm and counting 1-2-1-2..., etc.

51. SIDE ROLL KICKING WITH ONE ARM EXTENDED - PRACTICE ON EACH SIDE

Your brain has a built in compass and level to keep your body in balance. Put your body into this position to see and feel what the arm pattern will be like pulling when swimming. Practice on both sides.

For this step extend one arm on the bottom directly forward, rest on your side, and do the same kick you did lying flat. Learn how your body rolls when you're actually swimming so that your feet and legs will also stay somewhat together kicking on each side and stroking, too. Do not over kick, but allow your feet and lower legs to separate only 6-8" off the imaginary midline to reduce resistance and be more efficient. When swimming, your feet may separate 12-18 inches.

52. KICKING ON YOUR SIDE ONE ARM STROKING - PRACTICE ON EACH SIDE

Repeat the previous step and use your top arm to pretend you are swimming to coordinate with your kick. Do an elliptical stroke with your free hand and bent forearm while resting on your non-breathing arm side initially. Once you master that skill roll onto your breathing side arm, continue to kick moderately, and practice stroking with your other arm. You get the sensation of being level on each side while stroking and maintaining a moderate kick at the same time. This is designed to transfer the same identical elements from home to the shallow end of the pool.

53. RHYTHM KICKING ANKLES OFF THE MATTRESS

Extend your lower legs off the mattress so you will not feel the tops of your ankles beat down on the mattress. Keep your ankles and legs together so they do not overly separate and go outside of the midline to create resistance. Keep a moderate natural rhythm. This will make your transition to the water much easier.

54. CHILD GUIDANCE- FISHING ROD FLIP

For parents, place two fingers above and below your child's kneecap, and use your thumb as a brake to prevent his lower leg from lifting up too far out of the water or off the mattress. You can also press your thumb into the lower leg as if you were casting with your fishing rod to initiate the rhythm, and count out loud for them to hear 1-2-1-2 for a moderate kick. Do not allow large splashing kicks. You can cast the lower leg with your two fingers, and quickly press the lower leg back down with your thumb to create the moderate rhythm.

Ch.11 Bath tub progression

55. ON STOMACH FACE IN CUPPED HANDS

Your bathtub is a perfect place to practice. You may have to bend your legs to be able to get your torso in the water if you're very tall, and you can place your face in your hands to practice getting used to having your nose in the water. Now you can repeat the kitchen sink steps.

I want to caution you not to overfill your bathtub. When you lie in the tub your torso will displace that much more water that can cascade over the side of your tub and ruin your flooring.

56. REPEAT BLOWING BIG BUBBLES

With your face in your cupped hands you can either pinch your nose or get used to going without pinching your nose, and start to blow out big bubbles as you did before in the kitchen sink. Focus on opening your mouth a little wider. Then slowly exhale a large quantity of air to feel larger bubbles form out of your mouth and go up and over your cheeks. Feel the difference between small and large bubbles.

57. ON YOUR BACK LET YOUR ARMS FLOAT UP BY YOUR SIDES

This may not be a problem for your child, but you may have to bend your knees to lift up your legs in order to fit your torso flat in the tub. Hold your arms at your sides. Then totally relax both arms to let them float freely to the surface. Feel how your body parts can float.

By learning that your parts float, you realize that you are part of the problem by interfering and being stiff in your musculature. You also teach yourself mind control over your body parts to send a correct message to your muscles to relax or to increase power. Either way this involves controlling your body parts with your mind, and is an important step to master.

58. ON YOUR BACK - DEEP INHALE AND EXHALE

With your torso lying flat on the tub floor, inhale slowly, and feel your chest rise. Then slowly exhale to feel your chest start to fall. Repeat this several times to realize that if you inflate your lungs you will be floating. Then when you go to the pool, stand on the bottom and lower your torso up to your shoulders or lie on one of the steps. You can repeat the same identical element floating in your tub to develop your confidence.

59. MODERATE KICK ON YOUR STOMACH

This step will be easier for your child to perform in the tub than you. Repeat the same moderate rhythm kick that you did bouncing your ankles off the mattress. For children, use the shower curtain so that they don't splash water out of the tub. Children can get very vigorous and overly kick their ankles. Remind him to do only a moderate kick keeping his ankles and legs closer together as if he were kicking inside of a 5 gallon bucket.

Condition a moderate kick to feel the rhythm and be able to keep your feet on the surface without dragging your legs down to be inefficient. Your mind has to condition what your body parts do to get spatial awareness, and know where each body part is at any given moment.

60. MODERATE KICK ON YOUR BACK

Adults can sit in the tub and hopefully your legs are not longer than your tub to observe your kick. You can see and feel what you are doing at the same time to know that your feet are kicking as if they were in a 5 gallon bucket and not overly separate. Rather than point your toes to plantar flex your ankle, let your ankles relax so that the water pressure turns your feet into flippers. Only your toes will chip the water surface.

61. ON YOUR SIDE ONE-ARMED WINDMILL - PRACTICE ON EACH SIDE

Repeat the mattress step lying on one side, but bend your knees up to fit in the tub. Try to stroke one hand in the water to feel some water pressure.

62. ON YOUR SIDE ONE-ARM WINDMILL WITH MODERATE KICK

Do the previous step one-arm windmill and moderately alternate your ankles from side to side in a moderate kick.

This is a great way for small children to learn the rhythm of their kick along with stroking their arm. Be sure to practice on both sides.

63. ON YOUR SIDE ONE-ARMED WINDMILL WITH BREATHING TO BLOW BIG BUBBLES

Where possible try to roll your body and face into the water, and blow large bubbles as you repeat the previous step. This is ideal for conditioning breathing sequences for young children without having to be in the swimming pool. Then when you go to the pool, you can make the transition much more easily. Again, you will place your hand in the water to feel some kind of water pressure on your hand and forearm, but not stroke so hard that you splash water out of the tub.

64. CHILD GUIDANCE - FISHING ROD FLIP FOR THE KICK; TWO FINGERS HOLD THE WRIST OF THE STROKING ARM (DO SAME LYING IN THE TUB AS ON POOL SIDE)

Hold your child's wrists between your index and middle fingers, and thumb to guide him through the arm pull pattern. Make sure that he completes each stroke and lifts his shoulder, arm, and hand up out of the water or the tub. You can also practice the fishing rod flip in the tub as you did on the mattress, and monitor these initial patterns to master them.

To focus on lifting the hand and arm up out of the water, ask him to reach up to touch the ceiling or grab a cloud out of the sky.

Ch. 12 Transfer identical elements – home to shallow end of the pool in waist deep water

Waist deep for the learner and not the parent is appropriate. Then work next to the wall for added security. Use the ladder or steps. The steps work great to get the right depth and practice the same steps you learned at home in sequence.

This may seem too repetitious, but the motor patterns are still being formed adding the associations from the pool. As beginners become more familiar with simple tasks, they build their confidence and become less apprehensive to learn each new step.

Use caution. Do not become overly confident. You must be able to swim across the entire width of the shallow end pretending it is as deep as the deep end of the pool where you will not be able to put your feet on the bottom to stand up.

++++++

If you like this book, please tell your friends on social media and write a positive review on Amazon to help save more lives.

Here is a fast-link to find your book to write your review:

http://www.LearnToSwimProgram.com/Amazon-Reviews

Printed in Great Britain
by Amazon